Professional Cheerleading 21-Day Audition Prep Crash Course to Becoming an Arena Cheerleader for NFL®, NBA®, and Other Pro Cheer Teams

Written by an Industry Expert!

Flavia Berys

Published by

A Division of Cabri LLC
www.cabrimedia.com
Los Angeles County, California

Copyright © 2012-2013 Flavia Berys. All rights reserved. Copyright to all images used in this book belong to their respective owners. No part of this work may be reproduced, published, or transmitted electronically without express written permission from the publisher.

First Printing, 2013

Printed in the United States of America

ISBN: 978-1-938944-02-4

Photo credits:

Author headshot by Richard Pecjak, www.sunset-productions.com.

Book cover photo of the NPSFL Enforcer Girl® used with the permission of the San Diego Enforcers, www.sandiegoenforcers.com. Photograph by Michael Manzano. The Enforcer Girl cover model is Alexis Rodriguez, who currently dances for the San Diego Enforcers and is also the team's Dance Director. She works as an Admissions Operations Coordinator. Her top audition tip is "Have fun!"

Thank you for your purchase of this book!

As a special **Thank You Gift** to you, you can download some of the checklists and worksheets related to the content of this book as Microsoft Word® and Adobe Acrobat® PDF files for FREE after joining the Arena Cheerleading mailing list. The files can be downloaded and saved to your computer so that you can edit and customize them for your own use!

You will also find extra **BONUS** material such as:

- A video tutorial showing you how to apply arena cheerleader makeup,
- A special report and recipe booklet teaching you how to start your day with better nutrition, and
- Even more bonuses to thank you for purchasing this book!

Please visit **www.ArenaCheerleader.com** right now to join the mailing list and access your FREE gifts under the "BOOK EXTRAS" tab!

Need your help with Amazon!

If you love this book, please don't forget to leave a review at **Amazon.com**! Your review will help make the next edition even better! Every one of the reviews is read, and it really means a lot to get feedback from you, the reader. Success stories are the best of all!

If you left a review on Amazon for this book, simply forward the email from Amazon confirming that your review went live to receive a FREE 15-minute Q&A telephone call with Flavia Berys herself or one of her alumni pro cheerleader community members!

Just forward your Amazon review confirmation email to:

email@ArenaCheerleader.com

and someone will get back to you within 72 hours to schedule your telephone appointment!

Thanks again for purchasing this book and good luck at auditions!

Cheers!

About the Author

Flavia Berys is an experienced judge and organizer for professional cheerleading auditions worldwide. *The Wall Street Journal*, Fox 6 San Diego, KFMB Channel 8 San Diego, *Muscle & Fitness Magazine*, *Woman's Digest*, *The La Jolla Light* and other media have featured stories about Flavia's involvement in the world of dance and cheerleading.

Her 20-year involvement in the sport includes three years as a UCLA Cheerleader, five years as an instructor for the Universal Cheerleaders Association (UCA), and two years cheering professionally for the NFL as a San Diego Charger Girl before taking her cheerleading career behind the scenes. Flavia coordinated the promotional appearances and transportation logistics for the 2002 and 2003 NFL Pro Bowl cheerleading programs in Honolulu, Hawaii, where she had the opportunity to meet and work with cheerleaders from almost every NFL football team as an Associate Producer for e2k Sports. She was also hired by e2k sports to direct the San Diego Sockers Performance Team, a professional co-ed stunt squad, for two seasons.

Flavia also directed and choreographed the halftime shows for the 2000, 2001, and 2002 San Diego Jr. Charger Girl Programs, and organized and administered a series of youth cheerleading clinics on the island of Guam. She was contracted by e2k Sports to travel internationally to Prague, Czech Republic, where she directed Eastern Europe's first professional cheerleading team, the Eurotel Cheerleaders, which was later renamed the Chilli Cheerleaders. She serves as the executive advisor to professional cheerleading teams such as the San Diego Enforcer Girls in the NPSFL football league. She has worked as an expert witness for trials involving cheerleading negligence litigation, and is the author of other upcoming cheerleading books, *Pom Poms in Prague: A True Story* and *Professional Cheerleading: A Director's Guide to Starting, Managing, and Marketing an Arena Cheerleader Dance Team*.

Aside from her cheer-related career, Flavia is an attorney, business coach, and real estate broker. She teaches as an adjunct professor at California Western School of Law and San Diego City College. Flavia is available as a motivational speaker and executive consultant. Connect with her at **flavia@berys.com**.

Other books by Flavia Berys

Professional Cheerleading Audition Secrets: How To Become an Arena Cheerleader for NFL®, NBA®, and Other Pro Cheer Teams

This book became the **#1 Amazon Best Seller** in its category! This book breaks down the pro dance team audition process to give you the courage and confidence to show up on the day of auditions, as well as critical success tips to help you get selected! At almost 300 pages long, it is more comprehensive than the 21-Day Audition Prep Crash Course and best for women who have several months or longer to prepare for auditions.

Professional Cheerleading Audition Prep Workbook: A Companion Guide to the Audition Secrets Book

This workbook is a companion guide to the Audition Secrets book you are now reading. It is a step-by-step spiral bound workbook that you can use to write down goals, ideas, and to track your progress. It has all the checklists and worksheets you need on your preparation journey.

Upcoming books by Flavia Berys

Pom Poms in Prague: A True Story

This is the true story of exporting American-style pro cheerleading to the Czech Republic and chronicles the journey of the Czech women who bravely pioneered this new-to-Eastern Europe dance style. Join the **www.ArenaCheerleader.com** mailing list to be notified when it is published. (Coming soon in 2014)

Professional Cheerleading: A Director's Guide to Starting, Managing, and Marketing an Arena Cheerleader Dance Team

This guide will help pro dance team directors navigate the legal, practical, and logistical issues related to arena dance team management. (Coming soon in 2014)

Call Me Atlantis
Fiction (Coming soon in 2014)

The Tangerine Thief and the Concubine
Fiction (Coming soon in 2014)

The Landlord Prep™ Instructional Manual Series for DIY Landlords
Real Estate Legal Guide (Coming soon in 2014)

Legal Notice & Disclaimer

Nothing contained in this book is to be considered medical, legal, or tax advice for your specific situation. The diet and nutrition information in this book has not been evaluated by the FDA and is not intended to treat, diagnose, cure or prevent any disease. This information is not intended as a substitute for the advice or medical care of your own physicians, attorneys, or tax advisors and you should consult with their own physicians, attorneys, or tax advisors prior to taking any personal action with respect to the information contained in this book. This book and all of its contents are intended for educational, entertainment and informational purposes only. The information in this book is believed to be reliable, but is presented without guaranty or warranty. By reading further, you agree to release the author and publisher from any damages or injury associated with your use of the material in this book. Some products mentioned in this book are under trademark or servicemark protection. Product and service names and terms are used only in an editorial fashion for educational purposes with no intent to infringe or dilute such trademarks. If links are provided to specific products, those links are for illustration purposes only and no warranty for such products or fitness for a particular purpose is implied. Such links may be affiliate links that compensate the publisher or author if a purchase is made through such link. Such products are available at a wide variety of retailers and no recommendation is made or implied to use any particular retailer. The opinions of the author do not necessarily reflect the opinions of the publisher.

Contents

Introduction 10
Step 1 of 21: Today's task: Study hall 13
Step 2 of 21: Today's task: Calendar time 14
Step 3 of 21: Today's task: Make your research efforts count 15
Step 4 of 21: Today's task: Correct your nutrition plan 17
Step 5 of 21: Today's task: Choreograph a solo routine 27
Step 6 of 21: Today's task: Brush up on sports knowledge 30
Step 7 of 21: Today's task: Rehearse your solo routine - self-critique (week 1) 31
Step 8 of 21: Today's task: Select your audition outfit for the dance portion 32
Step 9 of 21: Today's task: Select your audition outfit for the interview portion 42
Step 10 of 21: Today's task: Finalize your audition outfits for the dance and interview portions 46
Step 11 of 21: Today's task: Rehearse your solo routine - full out (week 2) 47
Step 12 of 21: Today's task: Practice makeup 48
Step 13 of 21: Today's task: Practice hair styling 52
Step 14 of 21: Today's task: Smile for the camera! 54
Step 15 of 21: Today's task: Rehearse your solo routine - like a pro (week 3) 56
Step 16 of 21: Today's task: Social media clean-up 57
Step 17 of 21: Today's task: Review your research and complete the application 58
Step 18 of 21: Today's task: Visualizing success! 60
Step 19 of 21: Today's task: Tan, defuzz and nails 62
Step 20 of 21: Today's task: Rehearse your solo routine - final polish (right before auditions) 63
Step 21 of 21: Today's task: Pack your bag for auditions! 65
BONUS SECTION: What to expect on the day of auditions 70
BONUS SECTION: After the audition 82
BONUS SECTION: Do not let fear get in your way! 84

Introduction

When I wrote and published the #1 Amazon Best Seller in its category, *Professional Cheerleading Audition Secrets: How To Become an Arena Cheerleader for NFL®, NBA®, and Other Pro Cheer Teams*, I was amazed and awed by the response from my readers.

Your stories came pouring in. For many aspiring pro cheerleaders, that book gave them the education and courage needed to embark on the unique journey of cheering for the pros. Every email made the efforts of publishing that book worthwhile.

The feedback was overwhelming in its honesty, openness, and emotion. I was contacted by women who have tried out for the team of their dreams multiple times and not yet made it past the first round of cuts. I heard from women who have struggled with figuring out how to look, what to say, and how to dance in a way that will WOW the judges.

I listened. I counseled women one-on-one. I interviewed hopeful candidates and gave my honest feedback. I heard your voices. My email inbox became a sounding board.

I started to see one topic come up more often than most. Many of you wrote to say something along the lines of, "LOVE your book...I'm on the fourth chapter and I've already learned so much. But I'm panicking because I didn't find your book until last week, and auditions are only TWO weeks away!! I want to get through the whole book and implement everything but I just don't have time... is there a shorter list of just the essentials you can give me??"

I understood the need for quick research and fast results. After all, my original book was almost 300 pages long and full of detailed action plans! I can see that book just a couple of weeks before auditions can cause panic—a busy woman cannot realistically be expected to even finish the lengthy text, much less put everything into action!

In various emails, I sent out shorter, abbreviated action lists of what women could do if they only had a couple of weeks to prepare. I boiled down the ideal prep process (which can take several months to implement) into a "crash course" of essentials and shortcuts.

Those emails and advice became the book you are now reading.

Is it better to read the almost 300 pages of in-depth prep advice in my original book? Of course! But when you are short on time, this book is designed to give you the shortest path possible to audition readiness.

I have over 20 years of experience in the cheerleading industry, including two years as an NFL cheerleader, and many years directing professional cheerleading teams in the US and overseas. I have made a career out of training and advising cheerleaders, cheerleading coaches, and pro dance team directors in several professional sports leagues.

My mission in this book is to share with you the critical success tips you need to know to QUICKLY prepare for auditions. I want you to do your very best out there!

Auditions are scary. Being judged by anyone is intimidating (that's why job interviews are nerve-wracking!) but when you multiply that feeling times the number of judges that evaluate you at a typical pro cheer tryout, the fear can be practically paralyzing!

So what's the cure for that paralysis? Preparation is the best antidote. Preparation ahead of time will help you avoid any last-minute scrambles right before auditions and will help you look, dance, sound, and feel better on the audition dance floor. Practice and knowledge are also important. By practicing, you will train your body to be in showmanship mode despite the fear. Knowledge of what to expect during the process will help you avoid the additional uncertainty you can feel when doing something new.

This book was written to help you practice, prepare, and learn the essentials before an arena cheerleading audition when you only have three short weeks (and only an hour or two each of those days!) to prep for the big day.

I break down the audition preparation process into 21 sequential action steps to help you reach your dreams. Each item can be accomplished in one to two hours, so even someone who has a full time job or busy schedule can use this checklist to accomplish at least one task per day until the day of the audition. That's why this is a 21-day crash course!

Some action items will take more time, some will take less time. Even though I list tasks in a specific order, feel free to adjust and move around the action items. You might also choose to ignore some tasks, add additional items, or to double up on one or another. For example, if you have the time to take a dance class every day and can do so in addition to the steps included in this book, do it! Or maybe you have two months to prepare, and can stretch out the process and get more done than someone who only has one month. You may also need to condense this action list into just two weeks, or even one week if you are short on time. Use the book as a flexible guide. As they say in cookbook recipes, "season to taste!"

So what are you waiting for? The sooner you start, the more time you have to prepare!

Are you ready? Let's begin!

Step 1 of 21
Today's task: Study hall

Although this book is designed to be followed over a 21-day period, you will need to read it cover to cover today before taking any additional steps. That will help you design your personal action plan. Take an hour or two today to read the entire book to get familiar with the upcoming tasks.

Tomorrow, you will use your calendar to plot out your tasks ahead of time for maximum efficiency during the next three weeks. The steps in this book do not need to be followed in the exact order they are written. You have a lot of flexibility in how you accomplish these tasks. Before you decide how you want to organize your upcoming weeks, you need to know what's in store.

So for today, just read! If you are a fast reader, then read it twice.

Step 2 of 21
Today's task: Calendar time

Today is your day to open your calendar and schedule anything that needs to happen during the next 21 days. You will make the phone calls today to get yourself on the calendars of anyone who will be helping you on your journey. So open up that calendar and start writing! Your first entry should be the day of auditions. Then go through this book chapter by chapter and start inserting tasks into each of the days. If any task requires an appointment, make that phone call now.

Depending on whether you plan to take every recommended step in this book, these tasks and appointments might include:

- Setting up hair appointments
- Booking tanning sessions
- Scheduling a photo shoot with a photographer (or a friend with a good camera!)
- Asking your dentist for a teeth whitening treatment appointment
- Deciding which chapter of this book you will do on certain days (feel free to mix and match the chapters!)
- Anything else you need to schedule and book

By the end of today's work, you should feel organized and finally in control of this process. You should have a calendar chock full of action steps, customized to you. Your 21-day makeover and prep adventure is ready to begin!

Step 3 of 21

Today's task: Make your research efforts count

As I explain in more detail in my original *Audition Secrets* book, the longer you prepare, the better you will do on audition day.

However, it is still possible to rock it out at auditions even with limited preparation time as long as you spend that time wisely!

As a first step, you need to understand a little about the team you are auditioning for. You should focus your pre-audition research on the following critical research tasks:

- Find out the exact date, location, and arrival time for auditions and for any pre-audition workshops offered by the team. Mark those in your calendar and count backwards to see how much time you have before each event.

- Obtain a copy of the team's cheerleading application (usually available online). Read through it to get an idea of what you will need for the application (e.g. photo, resume, etc.) and to see how the audition is structured. For example, the application packet will probably explain whether there are multiple rounds of auditioning or just one round, whether there is an interview portion, whether you need a solo routine, etc.

- Download and print out a copy of the team's photocard (if available) and several individual cheerleader profile pictures. Pick out current cheerleaders who have a look that is compatible with your own hair, coloring, and features.

- Read recent press releases about the sports organization to get an idea about current news stories.

- If the team website has a staff directory listing the coaches, team president, player names, etc., print this out.

Step 4 of 21

Today's task: Correct your nutrition plan

Cheerleading is for fit, athletic women, not skinny undernourished waifs! This is a power sport, and to be powerful you need some muscles and lots of energy!

Today's exercise is to give yourself an honest assessment about your fitness level. At auditions, your body's condition will be visible to the judges. Do you look athletic and toned? Do you have visibly lean arm, leg and stomach muscles?

If there is a layer of fat or puffiness hiding your body's optimal shape, you need to honestly admit this to yourself and do what you can to correct this in the limited time you have.

The goal is a lean, muscled, taut athletic image. Picture a female Olympic® ice figure skater—see how you can tell she is an athlete? You want to have that same athletic look.

Today, make a plan and commitment to improve your nutrition plan. If you take an hour or two to plan out what your meals will look like for the next few weeks until auditions, you will be much more successful than if you simply make a commitment to "eat healthier."

If you are vague, you might end up munching on a pastry or candy bar next time hunger strikes. But with a good plan, you won't even get to the "so hungry I'll eat whatever pops into view" mode. The key is to think ahead and always keep yourself properly fueled to avoid hunger and binge eating.

The worst thing you can do for your body is to starve yourself or to go on a fad diet to prepare for auditions. Those can weaken you and decrease your energy! Whatever you decide to do, make sure it's a plan that will keep you energized so that you have the strength and power you need for the day of auditions.

You might already know the best diet for you. Perhaps you once had a great nutrition regimen and it's only a matter of getting back on that plan. You know your body better than anyone, so if you have already experimented and found something that works, get back to that.

If you have generally been on a good plan already but know you haven't been strict enough, make a resolution to have fewer "cheat meals" and to stick to your plan better.

Need a suggestion for a nutrition plan? First, check with your doctor before changing anything in your diet, and see if your doctor confirms the tips below are appropriate for you and your body before trying out a new plan.

If you are short on time and can't do your own research, and if nothing you have tried before has produced good results yet, then please feel free to follow the plan I set out below, which I call the NoPro Plan™.

There's no magic formula that will work for everyone, but in my experience the tips below help most body types lose weight and inflammation quickly. It's called the NoPro Plan™ because it is centered around elimination of processed foods. "No processed" is shortened to "NoPro" so that you can constantly remind yourself to pick healthy **whole** foods over unhealthy processed ones.

If you are reading this 21-Day book instead of my longer Audition Secrets book, I'm guessing you are short on time and need to see results fast! Some nutrition plans can take months before you see results, but most people who cut out processed foods the way I'll teach you see results right away!

Today's lesson is to either create your own nutrition plan (based on what you already know works for you) or to learn and memorize the guidelines below. After today, you will need to stick to your plan strictly, and every time you feel like having a cheat meal, just picture yourself at auditions to find your willpower through inspiration!

The NoPro Plan

"No processed faux food!"

This plan is simple and effective. The basic concept is that you replace overprocessed "faux" foods with foods that are unprocessed or processed very little. Check with your doctor before trying this plan, and also modify it based on your own food allergies or sensitivities.

I divide this plan into three stages: **The NoPro Diet**™, the **NoPro Plan**™, and the **NoPro Life**™. The diet stage is for weight loss, the plan stage is for maintenance, and the life stage incorporates a more holistic regime which includes exercise, supplements, and long-term maintenance.

Because you are only a few weeks away from auditions, I don't recommend the diet stage. A diet can shock your system and could result in low energy if not done the right way. That's why I recommend the plan stage when you only have a few weeks to shift your nutrition habits. It is less of a shock to the system, but provides the anti-inflammatory and fat-burning effects that you need right now.

Someday I will write a more detailed description of the concepts, which could fill an entire book by itself. But for this chapter of the *21-Day Audition Prep Crash Course*, I'm going to give you enough information to make a real difference in just three short weeks!

Here are the simple abbreviated guidelines, plus a recipe sample guide:

- **Up your water intake!** Begin each day with a full glass of filtered water as soon as you wake up. Finish each day with at least one full glass before bed. During the day, drink a couple of liters of water in small doses throughout the day. Begin this as early in your prep journey as possible, so that your body will stabilize its hydration level by the time auditions are around the corner. Do not drink from cheap plastic bottles, as those have been linked to toxins and chemicals which can leach into your drinking water, possibly leading to cancer and obesity. Use a BPA-free Sigg® or CamelBak® bottle instead. My favorite is drinking from a large glass mason jar (yes, the kind used for canning!). When you first begin to maintain proper hydration, your body will at first retain a little extra water, especially if you were previously living slightly dehydrated all the time. But as soon as your hydration level stabilizes at "well hydrated," your body will shed a lot of stored water. Basically, it realizes you are no longer in drought conditions and that it can let that excess moisture go! Did you know that dehydration is sometimes interpreted by the body as a feeling of hunger or tiredness? When you are hydrated, you look better, you have more energy, your skin glows, and your stamina increases. You will also feel less hungry!

- **Detox your body.** For a gradual, daily detoxification, try this tonic, which I absolutely love: When drinking your daily water, add a splash of unsweetened pure 100% cranberry juice which is not from concentrate (read the label to make sure there was no sugar added and no additional fruit juices or corn syrup). Whole Foods, Trader Joe's, and most health food stores have this type of pure cranberry juice. You can start with a small splash, and work your way up to a teaspoon per 10 ounces of water. Add a squeeze of real lemon juice (from the fruit, not those plastic lemon squeeze bottles!). It tastes tart, but you get used to it! If you are brave and get used to the flavor, you can even add an additional splash of pure unfiltered apple cider vinegar (Bragg® brand is the only one to use and it is available at most grocery and health food stores). I once served this tonic to my girlfriends in chilled martini glasses with some frozen blueberries tossed in and a slice of lemon and cucumber on the rim of each glass! The tonic sounds odd, but it really clears out your system and makes you feel great. In her book titled *Fast Track Detox Diet,* author and nationally-known nutritionist Ann Louise Gittleman explains how cranberry water is a gentle, daily detoxification. She teaches how it provides four organic acids that act as digestive enzymes to help your body rid itself of small fatty deposits that get stuck in the lymphatic system and also supports liver function. Gittleman further explains how this juice aids in flushing toxic fluids from the body, which can amount to shedding up to 15 pounds of extra water weight previously trapped in your body's tissues. If you are interested in the science behind this tonic, read Gittleman's book, the *Fast Track Detox Diet.*

- **Get your ZZZZZZZs!** In our sometimes hectic lives, it's easy to sacrifice sleep in order to get everything done and to enjoy a little free time. Most people spend their extra time unwinding in front of the television or playing video games, or socializing on Facebook® or other social media. But ask yourself— how many hours of time are you devoting to leisure that you could instead devote to sleep? If you are getting fewer than seven hours of sleep per night, try to adjust your activities and choices so that you sleep a full seven to nine hours per night. If you have been previously sleep-deprived (whether you realized it or not), the energy and wellness boost you will feel once you are well-rested will amaze you! Try to go to bed and wake up at the same time every day, rather than changing your schedule on your days off. Consistency is key—you are training your body to fall into deep and restorative sleep each night. Unbelievably, the extra ZZZZZs will affect your metabolism and your body will burn more fat and store less of it. Even though sleep doesn't seem related to nutrition, it is a huge part of how to train your body to perform and function better. So get your beauty rest! This will affect your mood, energy, dark circles, and stamina. Even though you would rather stay up every night rehearsing, don't!

- **Protein first thing in the morning.** Every morning, eat a high-protein breakfast within an hour of waking. Protein will set your blood sugar on the right path, which will help you make better choices for the rest of the day. It's also not going to create a sugar slump later, the way that a starchy or sugary breakfast would. The ideal protein breakfast can include some scrambled eggs, hard boiled eggs that you prepared earlier, some cold precooked chicken breast, or (my favorite) a protein smoothie. For three delicious protein recipes and a breakdown of what goes into the perfect protein smoothie, please check out the Special Report & Recipe Guide you can download for free from the ArenaCheerleader.com website. It's called *"What should a professional cheerleader eat for breakfast? And it's NOT Cheerios®!"* and you get a free copy of it when you join the Arena Cheerleader mailing list. I co-authored it with nutrition expert Grace Suh, who is a fantastic resource for nutrition coaching. It had to be cut out of this book due to size, but it is worth the read and I hope you make the breakfast switch. Download the report and recipes, tape it to your pantry door, and see how great you feel when you do breakfast right every day!

- **Eat organic and avoid processed foods.** The trend to eat "organic" is not just good for the world, it's good for your body! By avoiding pesticides, added hormones, and toxins, your body will feel a lot better. Did you know that synthetic materials have been linked in many studies to cancer and auto-immune conditions? By consciously avoiding food preservatives, herbicides, pesticides, chemicals, synthetics, and highly processed foods—and choosing natural, organic foods instead—you cut some very dangerous elements out of your lifestyle. As a bonus, you will eat less in general. Hand in hand with eating organic is eating foods that are not processed—that's where the "NoPro" in the **NoPro**™ lifestyle comes from— "no processed" faux foods! The foods we tend to gorge ourselves on are very highly processed. They were designed to taste good. Candy bars, potato chips, cookies, cakes, cereal, and pastries send your taste buds and body chemistry into a downward spiral of gluttony and pleasure, causing you to over-eat and fill your body with sugar, chemicals, salt, and empty calories. By choosing to stick with organic, natural foods that are as unprocessed as possible, you will by default cut out a lot of these temptations and will soon lose your urge to indulge in them. Once you are firmly on a **NoPro**™ lifestyle, it will amaze you how little you miss those foods. And if you do inadvertently indulge, your body will likely even feel a little ill from eating those faux foods after having gone clean!

- **Don't eat a lot of starch and sugar.** Every time I see a television commercial for sandwich bread, I get a little upset with the food industry. Especially the one where a woman puts wheat bread in her cart and the voiceover gushes about her healthy lifestyle choices. Even whole grains, brown rice, and the starches advertised as "healthy" are still starches. They are sugar. We crave sugar, and so we crave starches. Pancakes, toast, baked potatoes, pasta, rice, pastries, and pizza dough—oh my! Delicious, right? Your brain thinks so, and your body craves the sugar rush of those comfort foods, but your long-term nutrition goals will be sabotaged if you fuel yourself with these mostly empty calories. The more you cut the "white" starches out of your diet, the better you will feel. It will be hard at first (sugar is an addiction) but over time you will lose the cravings and will love the way your body moves and feels. Here's how you do it: Cut ALL starchy carbs and refined sugar for the next few weeks. Keep whole grain carbs to a minimum (and cut those as well if you are able). This means no pasta, no rice, no potatoes, no bread, no sweets, no soda, no "hidden" sugars like salad dressings, and no artificial sweeteners. Here's a great list of replacements that you can substitute for the most common starchy treats:

- Instead of pizza dough, use eggplant disks that you can top with sauce and veggies for a pizza-like treat!
- Instead of cereal, have a small handful of mixed unsalted nuts and dried fruit.
- Instead of mashed potatoes, have mashed steamed cauliflower with some freshly-ground pepper and paprika sprinkled on it.
- Instead of crackers, use carrot sticks, cucumber slices, and zucchini spears to dip into hummus and yogurt dips.
- Instead of potato chips, bake some kale chips by laying leaves of kale on a baking sheet and putting them briefly in the oven until they are crispy, topped with some salt-free lemon pepper and thyme.
- Instead of rice, use quinoa as your grain (it has a very low glycemic index and is high in protein).
- Instead of soda, drink green tea or yerba maté, both rich in antioxidants. If you need the bubbles, try Perrier®, Pellegrino®, or La Croix® sparkling waters in the unsweetened flavors that use just fruit essence to give it some scent without the sodium or sugar.
- Instead of processed and sugary salad dressing, use plain olive oil and vinegar or lemon juice with freshly ground pepper.
- Instead of pasta, use boiled spaghetti squash and top with your favorite low-sugar pasta sauce.
- Instead of artificial sweeteners, try xylitol, which is better for you than sugar, honey, artificial sweeteners, and even agave sugar (which, despite its popularity as a sugar substitute, is still just sugar!).

- **Cut down on salt**. Cut sodium to an absolute minimum. You would be surprised to know exactly how much salt is added to processed foods. When you start reading labels, you will see that the sodium level in almost everything that is processed (even pasta sauce, roasted almonds, salad dressings, canned soup, etc.) is amazingly high. The typical American diet is practically pickling us with the level of salt most people ingest on a daily basis! It adds up. All of that salt makes people retain water and get puffy. It can dehydrate you. It can also kill your taste buds so that you forget how to savor the more subtle flavors in foods. Stop using the salt shaker, and start reading labels. You will love how you feel when your body stops getting a large dose of sodium each day!

Sample 3-day recipe plan

	DAY 1
Breakfast:	Two scrambled eggs with low-sodium, nitrate-free, organic turkey cold cuts sliced into strips and cooked with the eggs. One large mason jar's worth of filtered water. Cook the eggs in coconut or olive oil. Do not salt them!
Snack:	Small organic apple cut into slices with organic almond butter spread on them. One large mason jar's worth of filtered water.
Lunch:	Chicken breast on a bed of organic greens with cut-up veggies, drizzled in olive oil and balsamic vinegar, sprinkled with freshly-ground pepper and a handful of unsalted walnuts. One large mason jar's worth of filtered water.
Snack:	Carrot sticks dipped in organic hummus. One large mason jar's worth of filtered water.
Dinner:	Grilled salmon with lemon slice disks cooked on it, a small baked sweet potato, and spinach sauteed in olive oil. One large mason jar's worth of filtered water.
	DAY 2
Breakfast:	Make a protein smoothie with vegan protein powder (I like Vega One in French Vanilla), a handful of frozen blueberries, some powdered greens or fresh organic spinach, and whatever fresh fruits you have in your fridge. One large mason jar's worth of filtered water.
Snack:	A handful of unsalted and roasted pistachios. One large mason jar's worth of filtered water.
Lunch:	A whole organic avocado sliced in half and filled with low-sodium tuna salad. The tuna salad should be made with low-sodium canned tuna (packed in water) mixed with olive oil, fresh lemon juice, a touch of balsamic vinegar or apple cider vinegar, and cut up celery. One large mason jar's worth of filtered water.

Snack:	A pear sliced into quarters, with a piece of hard cheese such as Spanish manchego or parmesan (unless you are lactose intolerant) and a handful of unsalted almonds. One large mason jar's worth of filtered water.
Dinner:	A stir-fry made with cubed organic grass-fed beef, red peppers, and cut up eggplant pieces all sauteed together in coconut oil and sprinkled with a pepper and salt-free spice blend, such as the "Sunny Spain" and "Mural of Flavor" spice blends from Penzeys.com. One large mason jar's worth of filtered water. A handful of cut up organic strawberries with a dollop of unsweetened Greek yogurt for dessert.
DAY 3	
Breakfast:	Sauteed mixed red and green pepper blend (organic frozen is fine and easy to keep handy) cooked in coconut oil. Two eggs served on the veggies, either sunny-side-up, over-easy, or over-medium. One large mason jar's worth of filtered water.
Snack:	Two cups of organic cottage cheese and a piece of organic fruit of your choice. One large mason jar's worth of filtered water.
Lunch:	A chicken wrap wrapped with organic large-leaf lettuce instead of bread. Take grilled organic chicken breasts and lay them in the large lettuce leaves along with julienne-cut veggies, sprinkle with olive oil and lemon juice, then roll the filling up in the lettuce leaf and enjoy. One large mason jar's worth of filtered water.
Snack:	Organic cut-up zucchini strips, hand-dipped as you munch in a blend of apple cider vinegar and sesame oil with any salt-free spices stirred in. One large mason jar's worth of filtered water.
Dinner:	Shrimp kabobs grilled on a barbecue or in the broiler oven on metal or wooden skewers, with alternating mushrooms, cherry tomatoes, cubed squash, yellow peppers, and onions on each skewer, served with a side salad of organic greens dressed in olive oil and balsamic vinegar. One large mason jar's worth of filtered water.

KEEP IT UP!

The sample 3-day meal plan above should get you going. Now, come up with your own meal plans for days 4 and beyond by using the above as inspiration for your own clever NoPro™ recipes!

Best Success Tip:

Cook ahead! If you prepare most of your food on Sunday evening, including prep work such as chopping veggies and food shopping, you will be less likely to panic and eat take-out during the week because cooking will be a breeze each day.

Place all your cut-up veggies into casserole dishes with lids and keep them in the produce drawer in your fridge. Have all your meats divided into portion-appropriate sizes. Pre-cook enough chicken on Sunday to get you through Wednesday.

Have enough organic fruits on hand to keep your snacks easy and healthy. Buy protein powders and unsalted nuts in bulk. Enlist the help of your family and roommates— it is so much easier to eat well when everyone around you is making the same effort! Teamwork is a great thing.

The key thing to take away from today's chapter is this—pick a routine and stick with it! Improve your nutritional scorecard and you will see results. Make your plan today, and stick with it for the rest of your 21-day journey. Best of luck to you!

Step 5 of 21
Today's task: Choreograph a solo routine

You might be asked to perform a solo self-choreographed routine as part of the audition process. Some teams will not require this, and it usually occurs during a later round. However, some teams begin the process with a freestyle round, so you need to have something prepared in advance to address either scenario.

Review the audition application packet to determine whether a self-choreographed routine is mentioned, and whether there are any requirements or length guidelines.

If you are an experienced stage dancer and have attended many auditions, you can probably choreograph a great routine you are comfortable with. But for newbies, I will give you a simple formula below to help you get something choreographed. My *Audition Secrets* book goes into more detail about solo choreography, but since you have limited time, I suggest you focus on the following:

The first 8-count should be just clapping out to the music, step-touching from side to side with your feet. Arms hitting a "T" as you step out, and clapping over your head with straight arms when you come together on each side looks best for pro cheerleading. During this initial 8-count, you can focus on showmanship and beaming at the judges. It will also give you a few moments to breathe and get more comfortable before hitting your more difficult choreography.

- The second 8-count should have one big dramatic movement in it where you claim your floor space. For example, you can jump out into a pose with feet a little wider than shoulder-length apart and arms in a pose such as a high "V" or one arm in the air with the other wrapped around your shoulders or midsection. Add some sort of swivel, or hip movement, or shoulder shake, or other flirty move, and perhaps end this 8-count by flipping your hair forward over your head, so that you end up with your nose near one knee for the last count.

- On the third 8-count, flip your hair up with drama on the first count, and use the rest of the 8-count to move forward in some way toward the judges. This can be a shimmy forward, or you can take some two to three large strides forward, or a leap or turn that moves you forward.

- On the fourth 8-count, add some hip-hop moves. Watch some Beyoncé videos on Youtube® and pick out some moves that you can add to your routine. This is the 8-count where you can show power, a little diva attitude, and sharp motions to demonstrate your precision.

- On the fifth 8-count, try incorporating some hip movements. For inspiration here, check out a Shakira video on Youtube®. Here is where you can add sass and sensuality. Keep your facial expression smiling—the goal is to look like you are having fun, not like you are seducing the judges!

- On the sixth 8-count, add your best technical element. Perhaps it is a double-turn, or a leap, or something more difficult. Be sure to pick something you can do perfectly, and that isn't difficult enough to stress you out. It should be a move you have mastered. If you know how to do multiple fouettes or a double axel turn, by all means add those! Show off your skills here.

- On the seventh 8-count, add an 8-count of whichever 8-count above you had the most fun with. This can repeat an element you have already done. It can even be an exact copy of an 8-count above.

- On the eighth 8-count, turn and walk backwards towards the back of the stage or room for the first four counts, then spin and walk back to the front for the last four counts. Arms can get creative—run them up your sides as you walk back then downwards as you walk to the front, alternate them, fluff your hair, wrap them around yourself, clap in front of you, hit alternative high and low "V's" or any other arm combination.

- On count "one," hit a strong final pose. It should be one that would look great in a uniform team card. Your face should be facing the judges, or looking straight up. Your hair should not be covering your face. You should have a huge smile on your face for this pose.

Feel free to modify or to use your own choreography instead. This is just a do-it-by-the-numbers guideline to help get your choreography juices flowing. Sometimes candidates can over-analyze and stress about the choreography portion. If you tend to over-think things, just stick to my template and you will have something appropriate to show the judges!

Today's task was to choreograph the routine. Now you will need to rehearse it every day. One idea is to set your morning alarm to a song that has a great beat, then make dancing your routine for 5 minutes your first thing in the morning when you jump out of bed! Just be sure to stretch first, or just mark the moves so that you don't pull anything. Or do your routine a couple of times through each night before bed.

The last part of today's task is to designate at least two days per week on your calendar as full-out rehearsal days for your solo routine. You should rehearse your routine "full out," which means that you practice performing it at performance showmanship levels.

Occasionally, I will send sample choreography videos to the www.ArenaCheerleader.com mailing list. Join the list today to get in on those emailed videos! Some videos will also be posted to the Arena Cheerleader™ Facebook® page at www.facebook.com/ArenaCheerleader, so be sure to visit and hit "LIKE" today!

Step 6 of 21

Today's task: Brush up on sports knowledge

Many teams will incorporate sports rules knowledge questions into the interview portion of the audition, so you should learn or brush up on the basic rules before the day of auditions. Your knowledge level should be that of a team fan who attends many games, not necessarily that of a coach or player.

If you already have a good understanding of the rules of the sport, that's great! That's one less thing to do before auditions. But if you need a little refresher course (or even a first-time crash course), then simply pick up a copy of a book like Football for Dummies or Basketball for Dummies.

Skim through the chapters today. When finished, go to the team's website to see if there are recent press releases or other news about the team.

Step 7 of 21
Today's task: Rehearse your solo routine - self-critique (week 1)

Today, make it your goal to rehearse your solo routine that you choreographed earlier until that routine shines. You should be able to perform it "full out," as if on stage at a major dance competition.

Dance it "full-out" every time. Do not "mark" it; your goal is to use this session as a workout as well as to train your body to dance in full performance mode when you do these moves. Your smile should be a 1,000 watts bright! Each move should snap with power and energy.

Today's task is to rehearse your routine for at least two hours. Videotape yourself using your smart phone's video feature or borrowing a camera, then watch yourself at the end of the session to see where you can improve. If the video is not one you could proudly post somewhere public, then keep drilling that routine!

Step 8 of 21

Today's task: Select your audition outfit for the dance portion

You should put a lot of care and planning into what you will wear at auditions. You will likely be competing against professional dancers who have experience auditioning for dance teams. The look is polished and glamorous, so don't show up in the same outfit you might wear to the gym or grocery store; this is your chance to add pizzaz and flair!

I have seen very talented and beautiful dancers arrive at auditions in unflattering dancewear and get low scores because they looked forgettable next to a less-talented dancer whose grooming and attire made her shine and stand out.

If you have read my more extensive book, *Professional Cheerleading Auditions Secrets*, then you have already reviewed much of my advice below. I am repeating that chapter here almost word for word, because this part of your preparation is important enough that you should review this criteria and these ideas more than once as you decide what to wear to auditions.

Your task today is to look through your closet to see what you already have, and to find colors that work well for you. Then do a little online research and place some orders at internet retailers (make sure their return policy is good!) or head over to the mall today after reading this chapter.

Keep jewelry to a bare minimum (sparkly studs or large solitaire faux pearl earrings are the most flattering) and take out all body piercings. Practice covering up any tattoos with body paint or thick coverage foundation.

Top

Selecting your dance top should be your main focus of time and energy. This is where you aim to be unique and memorable. Your dance top is your calling card at auditions; many judges will refer to you by the color you are wearing, such as "the brunette with the yellow top with a fringe." Therefore, you should put a lot of care into what you choose to wear as your dance top.

Here are my thoughts on your different options:

- **Pro-dance-specific top.** There are companies that specialize in designing dancewear for professional cheerleaders. The pro teams use these companies to design and produce the teams' uniforms in bulk, but you can also purchase one-off uniforms to use for your audition. My favorites are Angela King Designs® and DallasWear®.

- **Generic dance top found online.** If you are on a budget, consider getting a dance top online from a retailer like Amazon® or eBay®, then customizing it to look unique. I have run several online searches, and the one search that seems to bring up the best matches for what you need for a dance audition is this one specific search on Amazon.com:

    + Go to Amazon.com

    + In the search box, first use the drop-down menu to select "Clothing and Accessories"

    + Then type in these exact words in this order: sexy dance crop top

    + Hit "Go" and browse some amazing dance tops!

- **Bathing suit.** Some candidates audition in bathing suit tops. This is fine as long as the top is comfortable to wear while dancing and doesn't come loose or slip upwards or to one side. Triangle-top string bikinis don't hold up too well, but halter-tops are usually up to the challenge. Bandeau tops can be difficult to keep in place unless there is a strap or string that goes up around the neck. It is sometimes more difficult to wear a bra under a bathing suit, so if you need extra lift from a bra or bra inserts, then perhaps a dance top with greater coverage than a bathing suit is preferable. If you do wear a bikini, be sure to snip off dangling strings to make it less obvious you have a bikini on, and to lessen the distraction that flying strings will cause. You should also consider using body-wear glue such as Hollywood Fashion Tape® double-sided adhesive strips or a spritz of hairspray between you and your top to help it stay in place during the dancing.

- **Sports bra.** Most sports bras are too plain to serve you well on audition day. You don't want to look sporty; you want to look glamorous. Think Las Vegas, not the tennis court! With that said, I have seen some sports bras transform into gorgeous dance tops with a little creative arts and crafts approach. If you are crafty and have sewing skills, you can turn an otherwise ordinary sports bra into an amazing dance top. To get inspired, visit the websites I linked above to see what your target look should be, then design a top out of a sports bra that you can wear at auditions. The first step is to gather or ruche the front so that it gathers into a V-shape at your bust, then work on embellishing the straps or neckline with some sparkle (see below).

- **Sparkle.** I highly recommend getting a top with sparkle already built in, or adding sparkle to it yourself. Metallic fabrics, rhinestones, sequins, beading, and satin piping can all add a touch of shine. Embellish your top so that you shine in the bright lights. Pick one element and stick with it. If you added rhinestones along the neckline, don't also add other sparkle. Pick one method of embellishment and stick to it to avoid making your top look too busy.

- **Cleavage.** Select a top with sweetheart, deep "V" or corset "U" shape to the neckline so that your neckline is enhanced. You want to show off your collarbones, shoulders, and bust to demonstrate to the judges that you would look just as athletic and sexy in the team uniform. Most professional cheerleading uniforms are designed to be bust-enhancing. To be seen from a distance, everything in the world of theater and entertainment must be exaggerated. But the bottom line is that you absolutely do NOT need to have naturally large breasts OR breast implants in order to fulfill your dream of dancing for the pros. Anyone who tells you differently is ill informed! Wearing the right undergarments can add several cup sizes and fullness to a woman's bust line.

+ **Bra selection**. Many bra manufacturers sell push-up bras that will create cleavage and add a cup size. Frederick's of Hollywood, Wonderbra, and Maidenform are three examples, but there's no shortage of great bras out there! I recommend a nude colored bra with removable pads (which means there are pockets where you can add additional padding). Having a bra with convertible straps makes it easier to fit it under different dance tops. Here's another tip: When in a dressing room, make sure to dance in the bra to make sure it is comfortable and doesn't restrict your movement during a dance routine! You are also testing to be sure nothing comes loose or pops out during sharp movements. Other women in the dressing room might stare at you if you dance in the common area of the fitting room, but ignore them and have a little fun with it!

+ **Silicone bra inserts.** Many dancers choose to wear silicone bra inserts. These are sometimes affectionately known as "chicken patties" because they resemble a raw chicken breast cutlet! These are soft, pliable bra padding that resemble breast tissue in weight and look. These are sometimes marketed as bra substitutes, but for dancing, these should be worn only in conjunction with a bra, not instead of a bra. Many are sold with an adhesive backing that sticks to your skin. This is recommended because it will prevent the tragic and accidental "flying saucer boobie." Yes, I have seen a chicken patty bra insert fly across the room when the dancer performed a tumbling pass. And yes, it was just as jaw-dropping as you are imagining. I can happily report she played it off and made it onto the squad, but not everyone is going to have that dancer's grace and composure under pressure!

- ✦ **Makeup enhancement**. Here's a little-known secret: You can use bronzer powder to enhance or even create cleavage and stomach muscles. This should be done subtly with a light hand, and definitely get a second opinion for your "artwork" before marching it out in front of the judges. The idea is to add some bronzer in a shade or two darker than your natural skin tone to create cleavage and muscles.

- **Sleeves.** Short sleeves or long sleeves, which will you choose? The answer depends on your arms. Are they toned and lightly muscled? Then go sleeveless or sleeved, your choice. If they are not at all toned, unusually skinny, or very heavily muscled, you might want to wear long sleeves to camouflage them for auditions. You want judges to notice your smile, dance technique, and overall presence. If your arms are noticeably more muscled or much skinnier than the average team member's, this can become a distraction and the one thing the judges remember about you. Keep their focus on YOU, not your arms!

- **Length.** Crop top or longer top, what's best for you? If you cover your stomach, judges will assume you have something to hide. A longer top will also visually shorten your torso, and make the small portion still showing at the bottom look wider than it actually is. For the average pro dancer body, I recommend a top that is cropped to just below your bust (where a sports bra would end). This creates the longest look from briefs to top, elongating the look of your stomach. I have seen some very slim women successfully pull off wearing longer tops that reach down to the bottom of their rib cages or which incorporate a fringe that reaches down past the top. If you have a personal coach or mentor, have them help you make a decision relative to your body type. But if in doubt, go with a crop top. If a couple of fabric strips hang down from a center-tied top, that's fine and a good look as well.

- **Color selection.** Color is where you get to have some fun and make a statement. Pick a bright, fun color that works with your skin tone. Electric blue, cherry red, canary yellow, emerald green, fuchsia, violet, and tangerine are examples of colors that really pop. Solid colors generally look better than patterns, but a pattern will sometimes work on women who have done everything else right. A zebra-striped top on a perfectly groomed candidate with a great body and superior dance skill will help judges remember her as a stand-out ("remember that one wearing the zebra stripes?") but the same shocking pattern could backfire if you were not otherwise fully prepared, by adding one more thing that looked slightly "off" about you. That's why I generally recommend sticking with one bright color that works with your personal complexion, but on occasion I have given a thumbs up to a fun or unique pattern.

- **Get opinions from others.** Not sure which top to wear? Deciding between several top contenders? Here's an idea! Visit the Arena Cheerleader™ Facebook® page at www.facebook.com/ArenaCheerleader. You can post several photos (please no more than four!) and ask the community members to help you pick the best one. You can see their comments, or tally up the number of "LIKES" each one generates. If I happen to be on the page that day, you will get my personal input as well! You can also reach out to your own community of friends and family for opinions.

Briefs

It can be terrifying to learn you will have to audition in front of strangers and other dancers wearing briefs, but don't let that fear make you avoid the issue and get stuck with wearing ill-fitting briefs on the day of auditions because you did not adequately prepare yourself. Shop early, and try various cuts until you find one that works for you.

- **Cut.** Your dance briefs should be high-cut. Wear your briefs up to your hipbones or just above the bones. Do not wear them low at your hip, which I have seen many women do. Briefs never look good worn that low when a woman is dancing. Remember, you are not standing in front of a mirror posing; you are in motion! Wearing your briefs below your hip bones will give the illusion of shorter legs and creates an odd "muffin top" roll in certain positions, even when the dancer is very slim. Even if you feel and believe that wearing your briefs low on your hips shows off your stomach, I have to tell you—in action, it is generally not flattering. Lastly, choose a V-shaped waistband to accentuate your stomach and lengthen your torso.

- **Boy-shorts.** Boy-shorts or bike shorts will shorten the look of your legs and also make your behind look large when you are lined up with other women in smaller briefs. Even though they feel like they cover more and thus make you feel less self-conscious, stick with a classic high-cut brief. If you wear shorts, the judges will assume you have something to hide.

- **Bathing suits.** If you are using a bathing suit as your top, then consider using the matching bathing suit bottom only if it has the same coverage as a typical dance brief. In most cases, you should stick to dance briefs in black or a solid color to go with your bikini top rather than using the bottoms that came with your bathing suit.

- **Thongs.** Do not opt for a thong or Brazilian style cut, even if your behind can sport this look and look good. It will send the wrong message to the judges, and you will stand out from the other candidates as "that woman in the thong." Choose a style with a little more coverage. Yes, I am mentioning this because I have seen someone wear one at an audition!

- **Skirts.** Avoid skirts and fringes unless you had a professional designer with pro cheer experience make your audition outfit. When done right, this can add to the visual appeal of an audition outfit, but I have seen it done wrong more times than I have seen it done right. This is no area for an amateur to dive into without expert assistance.

- **Color.** Stick with plain black as a rule, but matching your briefs to the color of your top is also a good option. Avoid patterns as a general rule.

- **Pins.** Use small safety pins to keep the top of your hosiery or tights just under and below the top of the briefs. Check to make sure that your hosiery or tights do not peek up over the top of your briefs even after intense dancing.

Shoes

Wear jazz shoes to the audition, preferably in nude coloring. Avoid sneakers, boots, bare feet, or other footwear unless you know for a fact that the returning veterans wear such footwear. If auditions are held on grass, you could opt to wear sleek white sneakers instead of jazz shoes, but be sure to also take your jazz shoes so that you can change footwear after you see what the returning veterans are wearing. Your footwear should match their footwear as closely as possible.

Why is the right hosiery your secret weapon?

The right hosiery will make your legs look fantastic and will camouflage your cellulite. If those two reasons aren't enough to make you want to try different brands to find the best one for you, I don't know what will! Here are some great hosiery tips for you:

- **Million-dollar tip!** My number one, million-dollar, "OMG, I can't believe I never knew this" trick for wearing hosiery and tights correctly for dance auditions is this: Always, always, always (I mean without exception) cut a 1" to 3" deep slit down from the top of the waistband, starting at your navel and cutting downward. Stop cutting just before the waistband changes to the sheerer material. Snip, snip! Some cheerleaders that I know even cut off the entire top of the waistband. By doing this, you get rid of the "muffin-top" producing tightness of the waistband, and you also make the hosiery easy to tuck into a V-shaped brief. Try it once and you will never again wear hosiery without first making the waistband slit.

- **Sheer.** Be sure that your hosiery or tights do not have a control top (i.e., avoid the look of wearing tan bike shorts; you do not want a line across your thighs). You also want only a very small cotton diamond in the panty area, because nothing should show outside of your dance briefs during kicks or when bending down, including control top material or white cotton panty area material.

- **Color selection.** Your hosiery should not be a mismatch. Match it to your stomach color. If you are tan, use tan hosiery. If you are pale, go with a matching tone. If you are dark-skinned, use darker shades. Do not wear tan hosiery hoping it will make you look tan if you have not first tanned the rest of your body to match. Do not wear off-white, black, or colored hosiery at a professional dance audition. Stick to a nude shade matching your skin tone as your best choice.

- **Shiny or matte?** In general, shinier tights will accentuate cellulite but will give your legs a great "oiled" look similar to when you wear lotion or suntan oil. Matte will generally camouflage larger thighs better by creating less reflection along your leg lines, but usually offers less snugness and support. Try both and see which works best for you! Taking photos or video and watching the results is sometimes a better way to gauge the look than to just see yourself in the mirror.

- **Best brands.** One of the best brands of hosiery for dancing is L'eggs Sheer Energy® in "all sheer" because it is a slightly shiny pantyhose with a firm elastic feel that hugs your skin snugly and gives you support. For a more matte look, No nonsense® in "sheer to waist" is a good option, but provides less support if flabbiness is an issue for you. Waitresses at the restaurant chain Hooters® wear either Peavey® Hosiery or Tamara® Hosiery, which are also two good options for you to try out (the Tamara® brand is generally rumored to be better quality than the Peavey® brand).

- **One layer or two?** I believe you should wear just one layer of hosiery or tights. However, some women feel that two layers provide greater support and cellulite control. Try wearing two layers to see what you think works for your body. If you wear two layers, keep in mind that the color will darken so choose the color accordingly. If you normally wear tan, you might opt for "light nude" if you are doubling up.

- **Baby powder.** A small amount of baby powder spread all over your legs can help your hose glide on with ease. This is an old ballet studio trick that really works. Especially if you are sweaty, a very light dusting of baby powder can help you slide the tights up your legs without needing to tug and pull as much.

- **Four extra pairs on the day of audition.** Once you find the hosiery or tights that make you feel and look your best, purchase many pairs. You will need them for rehearsing to prepare for auditions and on the day of auditions. Always carry at least four extra pairs with you to any audition. I personally carry even more than that in case someone else needs a pair; you can be the person to save the day for someone!

- **Carry hairspray and clear polish for tears.** In addition, carry hairspray and clear nail polish to stop snags and runs in their tracks. In a pinch, when you don't have time to change into new hosiery, you can apply a dab of nail polish or a squirt of hairspray to freeze the tear before it gets any bigger.

- **No socks, no leg warmers.** Don't wear socks or leg-warmers to the audition. If you choose to wear athletic shoes (even though I advise you to wear jazz shoes, not sneakers) then wear low socks that are hidden under the shoes and don't show.

Take photos in it to compare it to other outfits

If you are deciding between various options for your audition outfit, take photos or video of yourself dancing in each outfit to have a better idea of which one is most flattering on you while standing and also while in motion. Get a second opinion from your family and friends. Be objective and go with the one that makes you look and feel your best, not the one you personally like better for other reasons. For example, even if your favorite color is green, choose the yellow top if that is the one that makes you stand out the best.

Rehearse with it on many times

Once you have designed your perfect audition outfit, rehearse with it on many times until dancing in it feels like second nature. This will help you tremendously on the day of auditions.

The main thing

The key thing to take away from today's chapter is this—find an outfit that makes you feel gorgeous and gives you confidence, so that you will go out there and rock it! Set a date on your calendar to rehearse with the outfit on and to finalize any embellishing work (such as time-consuming rhinestoning or sewing).

Step 9 of 21

Today's task: Select your audition outfit for the interview portion

For many teams, you will wear a different outfit for the interview portion than your dancewear worn for the initial and final dance audition. For teams in smaller leagues, there might not be an interview or you might be interviewed in your dancewear, and so it's possible you will not need to have a separate interview outfit prepared. Be sure to check this out when researching the audition requirements for each particular team.

If the audition info sheet or application gives you interview attire instructions, follow it precisely. If the requirements state that you should wear a business suit, do not assume that a dress shirt and skirt would be appropriate. Wear a full suit, meaning a matching jacket over your shirt.

In general, you will want to look polished and professional. Specifically, this means keeping your attire as close to what you would wear to an interview for a corporate job as possible. There are some pointers below:

- **Attire definitions.** Some audition info sheets will describe the interview attire as, "dressy casual," or "business casual." Others will state, "business attire." Still others might state, "dress nicely." You may even see it described as, "cocktail attire." Unless you have been to the audition or are a mind reader, it's hard to know what each definition means! Here's a list of what to wear for each one:

  + **Casual:** This is the only designation that would allow you to consider denim, but if you are planning to wear denim, I would first contact the team director well in advance of the audition to ask if denim is appropriate. The response might help you decide. If you will wear denim, I would pair your jeans with very high heels or boots and a fashion-forward top worn under a blazer or shirt jacket. Dress up your denim by wearing classic jewelry like a strand of pearls or long necklaces draped around your neck. If you do not wear denim, then an A-line skirt paired with a nice top would be appropriate. Do not wear workout wear such as yoga pants and do not wear a tracksuit. Skirt length can be as short as the tips of your fingers when your arms hang loose.

  + **Dressy Casual:** This is similar to casual, but would include a simple daywear dress, such as a sheath dress in a flattering color. You can also wear slacks paired with a light sweater or knit top, or a skirt with a sheath or camisole top. Skirt length can be as short as for casual wear described above.

  + **Business Casual:** Business casual means workplace-appropriate. This means that you should choose an outfit that does not leave your shoulders bare, and the length of your skirt should not go above the tops of your knees. A safe bet would be a skirt or pair of slacks in a neutral color, paired with a button-down shirt in white or a bright color that flatters you. Stay away from tank tops and camisole tops.

  + **Business Attire:** When the attire specifies business attire, choose a business suit in a neutral color such as black, grey, brown, pinstripe, or taupe. Wear hosiery in a nude shade. If you are wearing black, then you may wear black sheer stockings, but otherwise stick to a nude sheer look. Your suit can be a pantsuit, skirt suit, or sheath dress. Wear your suit jacket to the audition. If you see that no other candidate is wearing a jacket, you can take it off before your turn in front of the judges. Wear a button-down shirt or a colorful top under your jacket. Keep the length of your skirt or dress just above your knees.

+ **Cocktail Attire:** This is where you can safely wear your "little black dress." You can also choose a dress with color or sparkle. The length can be shorter than the other attires described above. You can show a little leg here, but if your dress is short, consider keeping the top more modest to create balance. Separates are also a good choice, such as a pair of skinny slacks with a fashionable top.

+ **Evening Attire:** This is the same as cocktail attire described above.

- **Pantsuit, skirt suit or dress?** Many candidates agonize about whether to wear a skirt, pants, or a dress. If you have outfits available in all three, I would choose the dress or skirt. But pants are fine as long as they fit well and are the correct length (hitting your feet just below your ankles). I see a lot of too-tight outfits at auditions, so be sure that the fabric is not too tight around your hips and that your underwear lines do not show. Be sure to practice sitting down and standing back up to make sure your clothing does not need to be pulled down or adjusted in front of the judges, which is distracting.

- **Shoes.** The best shoes are black, brown, navy, or nude colored. You want them to blend in with the rest of your outfit. If you will wear shoes in a bright color, the color should match and coordinate with your outfit. Open-toed shoes are generally not appropriate in the workplace in a formal setting, but are fine to wear for a dance audition. Do not wear platforms that are very tall or shoes that are overly trendy. Do not wear clunky shoes that can make your feet look ungraceful. Do not wear shoes that have too much sparkle or metal fittings, because they can distract from the rest of your outfit and from you as the main focus. Do not wear clear Lucite shoes with a platform; those are too "Las Vegas" and are distracting. Remember, judges are easily distracted, so keep your footwear simple and flattering.

Today's task is to select an outfit from your closet or to go to a store or online retailer to find what you need. You might also have friends or family members (such as an aunt who is the same size as you) who can lend you an outfit.

Step 10 of 21

Today's task: Finalize your audition outfits for the dance and interview portions

Earlier, you researched and selected outfits for the dance and interview portions of your audition. Today, you should review those choices, try them both on, and make sure you have finalized all details, such as which hosiery you will wear with each outfit, body tape strips, proper bra selection, shoes, and all of the other small details. Do not leave any of that for the day before auditions.

Finalize your plan today, shop for any missing elements, and put the outfits away somewhere where you will not lose the pieces in the shuffle. It might help you to write out a list of all the elements of each outfit, including jewelry, socks, straps, pantyhose, safety pins, and other small details. That way you have a packing list you can use the night before auditions to make sure you did not forget to pack something important.

Step 11 of 21
Today's task: Rehearse your solo routine – full out (week 2)

Today is another full-out rehearsal for your solo routine. Again, like last time, the key is to dance it as if you are performing in public. This session is training for you to get your body and—most importantly!—your MIND in the right mode for performing.

If you do the hard work of dancing your solo routine full out, including some freestyle for the first two eight counts, and finishing with a great ending pose, then when you learn the audition routine on the big day, your body will be used to being in that full-out performance mode!

It will be a piece of cake to perform at full throttle at auditions if you do the work now.

So your mission today is to dance full out again for at least two hours!

Step 12 of 21
Today's task: Practice makeup

Spend today's time practicing how you will do your makeup for auditions. When you try a new look, take a photo of yourself to see how that makeup style will look to others and in photos. A camera is more reliable than a mirror, and lets you save looks you have created for future reference and reproduction.

You can do this at home, or head to your local Sephora® store or department store to use their makeup counter for your experiments. Another great place to experiment is M.A.C Cosmetics®.

The look is dramatic. For stage, you wear more makeup than you normally do and up close you will feel like you are wearing too much.

Here is a general guideline for creating a great professional cheerleader makeup look (this has been shortened from the more in-depth list of makeup tips in the *Professional Cheerleading Audition Secrets* Book):

- **Moisturizer.** Begin by making sure you have enough moisturizer on your face. You do not want to have dry skin cause your foundation to get flaky or for it to settle into fine lines caused by dry skin.

- **Concealer.** Use concealer for dark circles, in the inner corners of your eyes, at the outer corners of your lips, along the crease from nostrils to the corners of your lips, along the sides of your nostrils, at the outer corners of both eyes, and on any scars, moles, pimples, and red marks. Using a small brush similar to a paintbrush works best for dabbing and stroking concealer into place.

- **Foundation.** Choose a foundation with extra coverage for dance auditions. You do not want sheer or light coverage; this is the time to bring out the big guns! The idea is to create a flawless finish, like they wear on television. Your M.A.C Cosmetics® counter will have foundation formulas with this type of heavy coverage. Just be sure the color goes with your face and also matches your body.

- **Powder.** Finish off your foundation with a light dusting of a matching powder. You will use this powder throughout the day to combat shine when you get sweaty from dancing.

- **Brows.** Use a brow powder or pencil to define your brows. My favorite powder is Anastasia® for women with naturally-thin eyebrows, but I also really like Brow Zings by Benefit® because it contains a wax as well as a powder to tame thicker or unruly brows. Nothing will open up your eyes and give you a polished look more than having your eyebrows properly shaped. Avoid pencil-thin brows; the best brows are thicker towards your nose and end in graceful slim arches. Take a few minutes to tweeze these into shape and to get rid of stray hairs.

- **Eyeshadow.** Your eyeshadow should consist of at least three shades of color. One is a light shimmery color to use just under your eyebrows, another is a medium tone color to use along the crease and on the lid, and the third is a very dark deep color to use exclusively in the crease and along your lid line over your eyeliner. The third color can also be used over eyeliner under your eyes if you choose to create a smoky look.

- **Eyeliner.** The idea behind your audition makeup is to make your face stand out. Even if you normally don't use eyeliner, you should use it at auditions so that your eyes do not blend in to your face under the bright lights. Stick with matte neutrals like brown, black, and dark grey. If you have small eyes, one option is to apply a white or light pink liner to your lash lines just inside of where you apply the dark liner, but be careful not to get any liner in your eyes.

- **Sparkle.** For added pizzazz, use a glitter or sparkle element very sparingly to accent your face. Do not go overboard with sparkle, but a touch of it can give you a glamorous punch that will help you shine out on the dance floor!

- **False lashes.** Before putting on mascara, consider applying false lashes to your eyes for an ultra-glamorous and show-time-worthy look. These are not easy to apply, so be sure to practice gluing them on often before committing to using them on the day of audition. You should also practice dancing with false lashes to get used to the feeling long before the day of tryouts.

- **Lashes.** Whether or not you use false lashes, you will need to apply black or deep brown mascara to your lashes (or over your false lashes if you applied those). Use several coats, and be sure to avoid clumps by using an eyelash comb as necessary to separate any lashes that get stuck together. Waterproof mascara is best if you sweat heavily when exercising.

- **Bronzer.** While this step is only optional, many women look great with a light dusting of bronzer applied across their forehead, down the nose, and along each cheekbone for a sun-kissed look.

- **Cheeks.** You will want a soft rosy glow on the apple of each cheek. Brush on a powdered blush, but be sure not to create a doll-like look, so be sure to blend the color well into each cheek to avoid harsh lines. A rose or peach tone is best.

- **Lips.** The best bet for lipstick is to go with a deepest rose or a true red. When in doubt, choose red! Many teams actually require that their dancers wear red lipstick for consistency and visibility from the stands. My all-time favorite red that seems to work with most skin tones is Russian Red by M.A.C Cosmetics®. Another good choice is Charmed I'm Sure (Marilyn Monroe Collection) by M.A.C Cosmetics®. You will want to start with a lip liner to edge around your entire lips, then fill in with color, then finish with a stay-put gloss. One note of caution: Test your lipstick and gloss to ensure it is smudge-resistant by dragging a lock of hair across your lips and seeing whether your hair sticks to your lips or smudges the color onto your face. You also need to test to be sure your lipstick and gloss of choice do not come off on your teeth when you speak.

- **Interview portion.** Keep in mind that you might tone the makeup down slightly for the interview portion of the audition if it takes place separately from the dance portion. During an interview, you are generally closer to the judges and will need less makeup.

After you create your look, be sure to take photos to see whether you have used enough makeup. A flash camera will wash out your face and color the same way that bright lights at auditions will, so this will give you a good idea of whether your look is defined and dramatic enough for the stage.

Spend the last few minutes assessing whether you need to restock or purchase any items, like a better shade of lipstick of better concealer than what you already have. Finish off the day by ordering those missing items online at Sephora.com or your favorite retailer.

Do you want to see a **VIDEO TUTORIAL** of a woman applying arena cheerleader worthy makeup? Would seeing a before-and-after help you? If so, visit the Arena Cheerleader™ Facebook® page at www.facebook.com/ArenaCheerleader, hit "**LIKE**," and then click on the tab for "**VIDEOS**" to watch a video tutorial given by makeup artist Carla, who will show you step-by-step how to accomplish the right look as she applies makeup to her own face. She has the cutest accent and personality! Carla loves to help women create their makeup looks by teaching them about proper makeup application, so please be sure to leave her a "thank you" comment below her video when you view it!

Step 13 of 21
Today's task: Practice hair styling

Spend today practicing how you will style your hair for auditions. If you will use hot rollers, do that today. If you will do something else, such as straightening your hair, do a test run of that as well. Then, once your hair is styled today, rehearse with it down and loose, dancing your solo routine a few times through.

You want to test your hair to see how it feels to dance with it in that style, and to test whether your styling technique has staying power. Perhaps you need to use a little more spray or shine serum to make it look great even after dancing a full routine.

To find your right style, go to the website of the team you want to join. Determine which of the current team members has a hairstyle that would look great on your own features. Use that as a guide. Every haircut, color and style on the current team was approved by the team management, so you can't go wrong that way!

The best look is one you could see on the stage of a pageant like Miss USA® or Miss America®. Check out some pageant footage on Youtube.com ® to get hairstyle ideas.

Another way to find great looks is to analyze the hairstyles worn on local and national news programs by the younger female anchors and weather reporters. The stylists on news shows generally stick to loose hair with a polished look for the women aged in their 20's and early 30's, and most of these looks would work well at a professional cheerleading audition.

If you don't trust yourself to do your own hair and if you love the way your hair looks when you step out of the salon, then perhaps you should schedule a hair appointment now to be in your stylist's schedule for the day before or morning of auditions.

Now, take a photo of yourself with your audition hair in place and styled the way you want it. Keep that photo as a memory of your audition prep journey!

Step 14 of 21
Today's task: Smile for the camera!

Today is your day to either go through your photo collection and portfolio to select your best shot to submit with your audition application, or you can have a photo shoot today to take a new photo.

Having a professional photographer is best, but you can also have a friend or family member be your photographer. If you hire someone, check references and make sure that you have the photographer sign an agreement stating that he or she does not own the photos and cannot use them for other projects (and cannot sell them) unless the photographer has your written permission. A sample contract is included in the Audition Secrets book and also available at www.ArenaCheerleader.com to mailing list members.

You will want to follow the application instructions exactly. If it asks for a headshot, then don't send a full-length shot! Vice versa if it asks for a full-length photo. Also note whether it states if the photo should be in some type of attire, such as business attire.

Bright natural lighting that hits you in the face from an angle (such as sunrise or sunset) are the most flattering. Studio lighting is also good. For ideas, you can search on the Internet for images of headshots by running a search for "headshot" using an image search engine. You want yours to have a quality look and feel; avoid the "casual snapshot" look.

For full length shots, look at how models pose in fitness magazine photographs. Look at the swimsuit section of clothing catalogues or online stores. For more ideas, you can also look at the photos of the current squad members that the team posts online. Those are the type of poses and looks that work well.

Evaluate your practice photos against the professional ones you find. Be honest with yourself about what you can do to improve how you are posing, what your expression looks like, and your grooming. Keep improving as you get more comfortable being in front of the camera!

Smile or wear a sultry look based on which look suits you best. Try both! But when in doubt, go with an energetic and genuine smile. Do your hair the way you will wear it at auditions. Your makeup should be more natural than you will wear at auditions, but should still be flawless and accent your features.

Today's exercise will not only help you get a great shot for auditions, but will also serve as a rehearsal for getting ready and for posing (many auditions require you to pose in front of the judges before beginning your dance routine, so finding your most flattering leg and arm positions in various positions will help you prepare for that).

Again, a professional photo will look best! But if you take care to have good lighting and take enough shots, you probably will be able to take a good one on your own, even when working with an amateur photographer buddy! Now, smile for the camera!

Step 15 of 21
Today's task: Rehearse your solo routine - like a pro (week 3)

By now, your solo routine should feel easy and you should be able to perform it full-out at performance level without having to think about the choreography.

Use today's session as a major workout, and dance at maximum levels until you are exhausted! Then try to dance full-out while exhausted. Auditions will be a tiring event, so you want to test yourself and train yourself to dance despite extreme fatigue.

Sweat it out and burn it up! Make today's efforts really count.

Step 16 of 21
Today's task: Social media clean-up

Team management dreads the day when one of their cheerleaders might do or say something that will reflect poorly on the sports organization. A media blunder, or worse yet, a media scandal, can threaten the director's job and the reputation of the team.

Because of the possibility of these media and public relations nightmares, pro dance team directors are especially cautious about putting women on a dance team when there is a stronger-than-average chance the individual could put the team at risk. This means that you should look at your Facebook® page and other social media accounts objectively.

Delete any photos or posts about yourself that are inappropriate. If you would be embarrassed to show something to your boss or grandma, then it's probably inappropriate to have it up there. Spend today's time cleaning up your social media accounts. Just be careful not to get distracted and sidetracked by your friend's posts and comments! Stay focused!

Wrap up today's task by quickly warming up and stretching well, then do your solo dance routine full out for five minutes, in performance mode, with a smile, sharp movements, and confidence!

Step 17 of 21

Today's task: Review your research and complete the application

Today, you should revisit the team website to see if there is any new item of team-related news or press release posted, and to see if there is any updated information about auditions.

Review all of the news you have gathered about the team. This will help you prepare for any audition questions which might involve current events or team-related information.

Next, complete your application and resume today. Make a copy to keep for yourself so that you know what you turned in. It's best to complete this at home rather than filling it out while waiting in line the morning of auditions— you have enough to think about that morning without trying to remember all the dates of your past employment and writing paragraphs about yourself!

Be sure to follow application instructions to the "T." This means paying attention to any submission requirements. Be detail-oriented and fill it out completely, marking an "N/A" if something doesn't apply to you rather than leaving a vague blank.

Highlight any past cheer team experience, especially pro teams, media, or entertainment positions. You will want to describe your education background and your professional employment. Include mention of community involvement and any special awards and skills.

Some applications will allow you to attach a resume, while others will state that you must write everything onto the form itself. Again, pay attention to what is being asked of you and comply with all directions. Like with any job application, you are being judged on your skill in completing the paperwork properly and paying attention to detail.

You should prepare a 30-second introduction in which you state a salutation ("good evening"), your full name, your dance background (such as teams you were formerly on), your current profession (i.e. student, store manager, stay-at-home mom, teacher, actress, etc.), your hometown, and a "thank you" to the judges or expression of your excitement to be there tonight. You can mix it up and change the order of these elements, or substitute other personal tidbits in place of these suggestions. I have included an example personal introduction below:

> *"Good evening everyone, my name is Carla Smith. I'm a former dancer for the Newtown Teamsters, and have been dancing ballet for the last five years. I'm currently working as a project manager for a construction company. Newtown is my hometown, but I am excited to have moved here to Anytown last year and would love to become a part of the Anytown Dancers. Thank you for your time tonight."*

Practice giving this intro a few times.

Again, wrap up today's task by warming up and stretching, then doing your solo dance routine full out for five minutes!

Step 18 of 21
Today's task: Visualizing success!

Your mission today (should you wish to accept it) is to just sit and think! That's right. No running around, no shopping, no big decisions to make... no research, no phone calls, no choreographing. Today you just... dream. ☺

Find a quiet place where you feel peaceful and calm. Somewhere in your home is fine, but you can also choose a park, the beach, or anywhere else that makes you feel relaxed.

Take time today to visualize success. Imagine what it feels like to be in a room filled with other audition candidates. Then convert any nervousness that thought brings into excitement and confidence. Do this in your mind; this is all using the imagination.

Imagine a panel of judges sitting at tables in front of you. Then imagine their individual faces. See yourself making eye contact with each of them, and feel your face and smile beaming with energy and fun as you begin a dance routine for them.

Focus on how your body's going to feel as it performs the audition routine. Imagine that it is strong, graceful, and powerful in every dance move. Imagine that the showmanship talents of great performers like Beyonce, Shakira, Madonna, and Shania Twain are yours to access and mimic.

Let feelings of confidence, excitement, focus, joy and power flow through your mind as you picture yourself getting ready, walking around the audition location, registering at the tables, interacting with other candidates, warming up, learning choreography, and all other aspects of the audition.

Lastly, know in your heart that you can have a great audition that day. Go over that thought until you truly believe it, through and through.

Stay in this mode of meditation and dreamscaping for at least an hour of time. This is your day to focus on the important task of winning the mental game. Auditions are only partially physical—a big component is the ability to keep your head in the game and your energy level high. Confidence is the most flattering look you can have that day! Work on confidence ahead of time by rehearsing the optimal mental state.

You can do this!!

Step 19 of 21
Today's task: Tan, defuzz and nails

Today, work on your tan, depilatory tasks (waxing, shaving, or tweezing all unwanted hair such as face and stomach fuzz, underarms, and legs), teeth brightening, and polish your nails to a natural french, clear or pale nude color.

Tanning beds have been known to increase your risk for cancer, so a safer bet is to have a spray tan or airbrush tan applied, or to use a self-tanning cream at home. If you have never tanned before, then consider skipping this step because this is something you need to experiment with before the big day in case your skin reacts oddly or the color is not right on your particular skin.

Teeth brightening can be accomplished at home with a kit. Choose whichever brand your dentist recommends. If you have recently had your teeth professionally brightened, or if your teeth have no staining and are already super bright, you can skip this step.

Step 20 of 21

Today's task: Rehearse your solo routine – final polish (right before auditions)

You have been rehearsing this routine for weeks now, so by this time you should be able to perform your solo full out with absolutely no concentration! Today is show time!

Take a video of yourself dancing your solo routine and analyze your showmanship and confidence level. See where you can improve and try it again.

Today is all about polishing and perfection— toes pointed, arms strong and precise, posture lifted, and a million-watt smile!

Dance for a full two-hour prep session tonight. This is how you are also testing your stamina. Auditions can be long and tiring, so you need to be able to dance full out for multiple hours now to build up your endurance for the big day.

Make it count today. Dance full out. Dance your heart out; smile like you already made the team. Dance with joy, and let the music move you. Today should be fun!

Enjoy it fully so that your mind can come back to visit this moment when you are out in front of the judges later. It will help you reach this state of pure dance and showmanship even when you are nervous later while being judged.

Step 21 of 21

Today's task: Pack your bag for auditions!

Tomorrow is the big day! You need to spend the afternoon today prepping and packing.

Here is a packing list for you to use, which you can customize to fit your personal needs. If you want to download this list in a Microsoft Word® format (so that you can customize it) or Adobe® PDF format (so you can print it out), you can download it for free if you join the Arena Cheerleader™ mailing list at www.ArenaCheerleader.com.

- **Audition bag.** Pack everything into a duffel bag or small rolling suitcase. Do not show up with multiple bags or small bags hanging off of you. Fit all smaller bags, such as makeup bags and hair styling tool bags, into one large bag that consolidates everything you need. Be sure to attach a luggage tag with your name and phone number on it in case your bag gets lost.

- **Small baggage lock.** Bring one of those small combination suitcase locks that are sold for airplane travel. Make sure it requires a combination that you can easily remember, not a key. You can use this to secure your bag during the audition. There are a lot of people at auditions, and you want to make sure your belongings are secure when you are not with your bag. If you have heard rumors of problems with theft at that particular audition, you may even want to bring a small cable like those used to lock up bicycles so you can secure your bag to a railing.

- **Warm-ups.** Wear a tracksuit or warm-ups over your audition outfit when you arrive. You can also put this on later to stay warm between rounds.
- **Clear packing tape.** You will likely be given an audition number that you will pin onto your outfit. In case this number tears or starts to get wrinkled, you can use the clear packing tape to do some restoration work.
- **Safety pins.** This is for your number in case you are not provided with enough pins, as well as emergency outfit repairs.
- **Bottled water.** Bring much more water than you think you will need. Remember, you will be dancing all day, and dehydration can sneak up on you and zap your energy. Don't count on drinking fountains being conveniently near or available. You do not want to waste practice time waiting in the line for the drinking fountain. It is also difficult to drink more than a few mouthfuls at a time when drinking from a fountain, and the water quality might be lacking.
- **Snacks.** Pack snacks that will not be messy to eat, and that will not give you a sugar crash. Unsalted nuts, protein bars, cut-up fruit, and canned protein smoothies make convenient and healthy snacks.
- **Mirror.** Bring a large mirror in case there are none provided or the public mirrors are crowded.
- **Makeup.** Bring your full set of makeup, not just touch-up items. Even bring your foundation, in case you have to wash your face and start from scratch due to excessive sweating during the preliminary round.
- **Hair tools and products.** Bring your full set of hair products (hair spray, shine spray, gel, mouse, etc.) and styling equipment (curling iron, flat iron, etc.).
- **Hot tool sleeve.** If you will bring a curling or flat iron, consider buying one of the heat-guard cover/sleeves that allows you to pack your curling or flat iron before it fully cools.
- **Tissues.** Bring tissues and baby wipes.

- **Backup outfit.** Bring your audition outfit, of course, but also a backup outfit in case you need to change. You can even bring two extra outfits, such as your "runners up" outfits that didn't make the final cut when you selected your final outfit from all of your options.

- **Hosiery.** Don't forget your tights or pantyhose! And bring several extra pairs. You will probably get at least one run that day.

- **Clear nail polish.** Bring some clear polish to dab onto pantyhose runs to stop them in their tracks if you don't have time to change them and the run is very small.

- **Toothbrush and toothpaste.** A box of mints is a good idea as well. Do not bring any chewing gum. Most people look tacky or unfriendly when chewing gum.

- **Deodorant.** Choose a clear "no mess" roll-on or solid over the spray kind. Get the kind that advertises "no white marks" so that you do not have powdery-looking armpits.

- **Small towel.** Like when going to the gym, a workout towel is a must for drying off sweat.

- **Music.** If you prepared a solo routine, throw a copy of your music on a CD into your bag, just in case you have the opportunity to perform it. You should also take it with you on a small thumb drive as an MP3 file if you can. You can also pack a small inexpensive MP3 player and headset to listen to it during your free warm-up time or during long wait times if you need something to calm your nerves. Be sure to remove the headset if you are within eyesight of the judges.

- **Identification.** Bring your identification and a copy of your medical insurance card. It is also a good idea to jot down any medication allergies on your insurance card copy in case of an emergency.

- **Cash.** Bring a small amount of cash to cover the application fee (if any) and contingencies like parking fees, lunch, and emergency cab fare.

- **Extra copy of your application.** Even if you sent your application in early, bring an extra copy of it with you, along with an extra headshot. If your application got lost in the shuffle somehow, you do not want to fill one out from scratch.

- **Extra shoes.** Bring an extra pair of dance shoes, in case the floor surface creates issues with your original pair or in case your original pair breaks.

- **Phone.** If you bring a cell phone, be aware that your belongings will probably not be secure or under your control while you are dancing. Think twice before bringing an expensive smart phone with you. Consider borrowing a less-expensive phone to have with you for the day of auditions to avoid major issues in case of theft.

That's it — you made it through the 21-day audition prep crash course!

Now get out there and SHINE!

Good luck at auditions!

I'm rooting for you!

(BONUS: Turn the page for special BONUS material!)

BONUS SECTION
What to expect on the day of auditions

Congratulations! You made it through the 21-Day Audition Prep process. In this bonus section, I will share with you what to expect and will give you great tips about how to wow the judges!

What are the typical components of a pro cheer audition?

Every team runs the audition process its own way, so there is no hard and fast rule about what to expect. Some teams even change their procedures from year to year. That's why you should always be prepared for any possibility. That way, you will not be caught off guard if the team does something unexpected.

Here are some typical audition elements:

- **Initial welcome.** The day will probably start with some sort of introduction. You will be told what to expect, how the day will run, and will likely hear the biographies for key personnel and the choreography instructor.
- **Warm-up.** There may be a group warm-up, or you might be instructed to warm up on your own. Be aware that you are already on display.

- **Choreography.** The group will probably be taught a group routine. Some teams may skip this and prefer to see only solo routines choreographed by each candidate. But the typical experience includes learning the same routine as every other candidate. Some of the staff members watching this portion might be judges—you never know. Even while learning, be sure to exude confidence and showmanship.

- **Practice.** Although you will feel like there wasn't enough time given to you for practice, you will have at least some time to practice and polish the steps before you are expected to perform for the judges. Many teams will also give you grooming touch-up time after or concurrent with the time designated for practice.

- **Judging.** The judging component is where you get to dance and perform in front of a panel of judges. This can be in groups of two or three, or solo by yourself, depending on how that team structures its audition format. You might be asked to dance with pom-poms or with bare hands, with an open public audience or no audience at all, in front of the other candidates or by yourself in a room separate from the other hopefuls, and you might have to perform the routine more than once. There might be videocameras in the room, so do not let that distract you. The format can vary from team to team and even year to year, so walk in with an open mind about what to expect.

- **Interviews.** Not all teams have formal interviews. Some teams' judges might just ask you a few questions right before or after the dance portion, with you standing out on the dance floor. Others might set up an interview room where you will sit in front of a panel of judges. Interviews can take place the same day as the preliminary audition, or might take place on a separate designated day. For the teams that include an interview portion, this might be solely for finalists who make it to a final round rather than for the entire pool of applicants. Brush up on your personal introduction, knowledge of current events, knowledge about the team and league, and general sports knowledge.

- **Solo routines.** Not all teams will require you to perform a solo routine. Like with interviews, this might be reserved only for the candidates who are selected for a final round. Some teams request that you wear a different outfit for your solo, while others will ask that you wear the same costume as you did for the group performance. This element can take place on the same day as the first round, or at a later date, such as the following day or a week later.

- **Final rounds.** Not all teams have a final round, because some teams will hold only one main round and one cut. It generally depends on the size of the turnout of candidates. The more applicants there are in relation to the size of the final team, the more rounds of cuts the team will probably make. The final round can consist of the same routine as the initial round, or a new routine. It might be the same routine from before, but with added 8-counts to make it longer. You might perform in groups of two or three, or solo, or a combination of group and solo work. Be prepared for anything, even impromptu interview questions when you take the floor.

- **Media interviews.** Do not be caught off guard if you see media in attendance. Local news stations, photographers, and newspaper reporters will probably be in attendance for the audition, especially if it is for a major league team. Never assume that you can quietly audition for the team without anyone at work or in your family finding out—it's very possible your family, friends, and coworkers will see you on the news that night! During registration, you will most likely have signed a liability waiver and photography release that gives the team the right to photograph you and use those photos on their website, in video, or to give other parties the right to those images.

- **Veteran candidates.** Some teams give veteran returning team members a "pass" on auditioning and allow the vets to remain on the squad without re-auditioning. Other teams make veterans audition side by side with new rookie candidates. Yet still other teams opt for a hybrid method, where veteran candidates can skip the first preliminary round, but may show up automatically at a later round. It is a good idea to find out which way the audition you attend is organized, so that you have a better feel for who's your competition. There is usually a lot of tension in the air when veteran candidates walk into the audition room for the first time when they were not there for the earlier round. Many candidates do not realize that veterans sometimes get to skip the early rounds, which gives a false sense of the talent level in the room at the start of the audition. It can throw people off their game to realize that they misjudged the number of top competitors. Here's an important note: Do not be intimidated by the returning veterans! Instead, LEARN from them by watching how they dance, how they interact, and how they carry themselves. You should emulate their body language and grooming as much as possible.

- **Additional post-audition cuts.** Some teams will select a group of women to join the squad, but will reserve the right to continue with cuts during a training period that could last a few weeks or the entire pre-season. For those teams, the audition doesn't truly end until the team's management announces that the cutting period is over. Other teams will only cut team members for good cause, such as absences or bad behavior.

How are auditions scored?

Scoring and judging methods vary from team to team. There is no standard method. On the Country Music Television reality series Dallas Cowboys Cheerleaders: Making the Team, which follows the audition process and making of the annual Dallas Cowboys Cheerleaders squad, the team director instructs judges to score each candidate with either a "yes," "no," or "maybe." Other teams follow a similar format. Some teams use numerical scoring instead, which can be on a 1-10 or 1-5 scale. Yet others follow other scoring conventions.

Some team directors choose not to use scores at all, but have the judges write down only notes and comments. Some teams are selected subjectively based on discussion among management and judges, while others weigh the numerical scores heavier when selecting or whittling down the candidates.

For teams that use numerical scoring systems, the judges might give one overall number for each candidate, or might give separate numerical scores for specific categories, such as one score for dance and another for grooming. The formulas for averaging the scores between categories, and the decision to weigh one category higher than another (for example, whether to weigh a dance score higher than an appearance score), also varies depending on what the team's management decides to do that year.

The main takeaway here is that you should NOT agonize over how the selection system will work at your particular audition. Chances are, the system is not publicly described like the one on the Dallas show, so you might never know exactly how the final decisions are made.

You should focus on doing your own personal absolute best, and don't stress over how the scoring and selection technicalities operate. Even if you know how they work, it would be extremely difficult to successfully "game" the system or have an advantage simply by knowing how the decision process works. Your best bet is to go out there and CRUSH IT, giving your top performance so that you increase your chances of getting selected, regardless of how the scoring is done.

Lots of down time

Expect a lot of down time. Utilize your down time to rehearse the dance further, chat with other candidates, stretch, and touch up hair and makeup. Do not let the down time make you nervous, and use that time to drink water so that you remain hydrated, and to eat snacks so that you keep your energy level up.

Always be in audition mode

Your audition begins when you are within eyesight of the audition location. You are always on display, even during break times and the warm-up period. Keep in mind that you are being judged at all times.

This means that every minute counts, even when you are at the registration table. You should be as friendly and polite to the staff person who checks you in and gives you your number as you are to the judges. The registration staff might have the direct ear of the team director. For all you know, the team's choreographer was the person who checked you in!

Do not chew gum or chat loudly on your cell phone around other people. Gum chewing makes a person seem less classy, and it can also make you look unfriendly. Speaking loudly on a cell phone in public can appear rude.

All members of the organization, photographers, media personnel, and other co-applicants should be treated with courtesy and respect. Always be polite; you never know who's watching!

Learning the choreography

The choreography will likely be taught at a fast pace. This can make a lot of dancers nervous. It is stressful enough to be on display in front of judges, but now you will have the added stress of speed-learning a complex dance routine.

Do your best to keep up, and try to keep your face positive and calm (even if you are frustrated and worried on the inside). Many judges preview the group during the learning portion, so it is important to stand out as a star even during this early part of the day.

Try to perform as full out as possible every time that the teacher has the group practice to music. Make it a rule that if the music is on, you are on 100%. It will tire you out more than just marking the steps, but it will help your body learn to automatically perform the dance in full-out game mode. If you practice weakly by marking it, you will probably end up looking less than 100% in front of the judges when it counts. If you prepared adequately before auditions by getting yourself in tip-top fitness condition, then it won't be as grueling to push yourself to go full out all day.

If your double-turn pirouettes are not clean and controlled, consider doing a single-turn pirouette instead where the routine includes turns. Be as precise in your arm and leg motions as possible. Be aware of placement for each position by watching the choreographer and teaching assistants carefully.

Be sure to use your shoulders and hips to add a flirty sass to the moves that call for it. Listen to the instructor. If she or he says that a certain move should be performed with attitude, be sure to add in some flair!

Keep your movements big, meaning that you should dance as if you own the space around you. Do not be bashful or timid with your motions. Every cell in your body should exude confidence and fun energy while you dance. For inspiration, do a search on Youtube.com for professional cheerleaders dancing at games. Many fans post videos of halftime and other performances. Watch how the cheerleaders mesmerize the crowd with their big, bold movement. Emulate it!

Small details, like pointing your toes and paying attention to your hand position, are critical. But your overall showmanship is far more important then the small details!

Why do your smile and body language matter so much?

The quality and genuineness of your smile are critical factors for your success. Your smile truly determines the impression you make on the judges. As a cheerleader on the team, you will be expected to smile for most of the time you are in the public eye. The judges want to know you can handle that responsibility and that you have the capacity to look joyful and excited even when under intense pressure.

A cheerleader who looks nervous during a halftime performance will not look right. Similarly, a face furrowed in deep concentration is not fun to watch either. Worse yet, no one wants to see a cheerleader who looks terrified! So avoid any of these expressions out on the dance floor.

But a smile without confident body language cannot look genuine, so you are going to have to address how you stand, walk, and speak during the entire audition process.

So I'm going to share a secret weapon with you about body language. It's an amazing and effective tool. I've been using this technique for much of my life, but never really realized that I did, or understood the reason it works so well, until I heard a presentation about it by social psychologist Amy Cuddy. Her research on body language reveals that we can change other people's perceptions—and even our own body chemistry—simply by changing body positions.

You heard that right; you can change how you feel by first changing how you are standing. Amy teaches how "power posing"—standing in a posture of confidence, even when we don't feel confident—can affect testosterone and cortisol levels in the brain. She explains, "Don't fake it 'till you make it. Fake it 'till you become it." If you want to learn the science behind this theory, listen to her TED® Talk titled *"Your body language shapes who you are."* It is 20 minutes long and worth every minute, but if you are short on time, then I suggest you at least watch from the 17:00 mark for the last three minutes.

If you practice nothing else before auditions, practice smiling while under stress. Also practice walking, standing, and speaking with confidence even when you feel scared or intimidated inside. Like Amy teaches, fake it 'till you BECOME it! It's harder than one might think, but a skill that will serve you well for life.

How your facial expressions can sabotage your performance

Before I cheered for the pros, I was an instructor for the Universal Cheerleaders Association. That job involved judging many high school cheer and dance competitions. I was an instructor for several years, and over those years I witnessed an evolution in the facial expressions cheerleaders and dancers used during routines.

Somehow, it became in style to add scowls, power play movements like bicep flexing and air slashing, and even some movements that I could have sworn looked like something a mobster on television would motion to offend another character on the show. In addition to these odd menacing "we are number one and you better step off" type dominance body language, I also saw an increase in exaggerated winking, open mouthed surprised expressions, shocked faces, attitude, "kissy-face," pouting, goofy sticking out of tongues, and just general "over-acting."

Because this type of facial play became so common at the high school level, I did see some spill over into the pro world at auditions. Needless to say, most of this does not go over well at a professional-level audition.

Go easy on adding facial expressions. Your performance should be at least 90% smiling, with the other 10% adding a little bit of sass in the form of opening your smile wider for a moment or two, or perhaps winking once or twice in your entire routine. Keep it mainly "smiles" and you won't have to worry about coming across as "over the top" or silly.

The last type of facial expression that you should never show is to lip sync along to the song. I have seen this a few times, and it never looks good. An arena cheerleading audition is not an air band routine or karaoke. Do not act like a rock star, because the judges are not looking for pop stars—never sing along to the song while you dance.

Should you show off your gymnastics?

Showing off gymnastics skills at an audition is a tricky thing. It can easily backfire on you. I recommend doing one clean pass (such as a series of back-handsprings or an aerial cartwheel) during your entrance or solo ONLY if you can nail it consistently and gracefully, have no issues on hard floors, and can perform well under pressure.

I have also seen a successful single back-handspring or standing back-tuck performed during the "freestyle" portion of a group audition routine. Those work well when the candidate lands cleanly and immediately picks up with the dance movements. This is not the time to whip out your rusty grade-school gymnastics skills. If you are not in current practice, don't risk the possibility of injury, a shaky landing, distance misjudging, or general awkwardness.

If you are an experienced gymnast and decide to perform gymnastics at the audition, don't show off your toughest trick. Stick to something clean and reliable. To many of the judges, a series of three back-handsprings will look just as impressive as a double-full layout. Many will not have the eye or experience to differentiate between the different gymnastics flips, so stick to whatever you can do without concentrating too hard. Believe me, you will need your focus for the next stage! I have seen candidates freeze after throwing a tumbling pass, forgetting the audition routine because they were so focused on the gymnastics. Don't let that be you!

Top tip for what to do when your turn on the floor is only minutes away

One of the most terrifying moments during an audition is that one- to four-minute period when you are almost to the front of the line during the solo or small group portion. For many dancers, this is the time when the world starts closing in, heartbeats get frantic, and breathing becomes difficult. You watch as the number of women in front of you dwindles to nothing, knowing you are next on the floor, your entrance mere seconds away. You might even have this flashing thought, "What would happen if I make a run for the door and never look back?"

My top tip for that moment is this:

> **First**, take a deep breathe.
>
> **Second**, pull your shoulders back and stand in a pose of confidence, whether you feel it yet or not.
>
> **Third**, get that performance smile on your face, even if it is a few minutes early. And keep it there until it's your turn to enter.
>
> **Last**, in those last couple of minutes, look at the judges. Watch their faces. Face your fears, and know that those faces will be watching you momentarily. Then tell yourself, "They want me to do my best. Those judges want every one of us out here to give our best audition. Nobody on that panel wants me to fail; everyone is supportive and rooting for me."

Create a feeling of excitement. Imagine that the judges know you personally, and that they know you are a great dancer and are excited to watch you perform for them. Imagine that you have friends at that table. And when you walk out there, smile at those friends, connect with them, and shine for them.

What to do during your floor entrance

Your entrance can be one of the most important parts of your audition. You are already on stage even when you are waiting for your entrance, such as when standing in line or being next in line. Personally, I jot down my first impression of a candidate while I watch each one come out onto the floor.

During your entrance, you have no choreography to worry about. You are not yet dancing or performing the 8-counts. You can concentrate less on dance steps and 100% on your presentation of your pure self.

Make your entrance shine. Don't walk timidly on and then turn it on only once the music starts... it is too late to make a first impression at that point. Instead, sashay your way gracefully onto the dance floor with a subtle jazz-style walk (pointed toes, light on your feet, shoulders up and back, stomach held tight, dazzling smile). Use your shoulders to communicate your confidence and energy. Exude the same energy you would show if you were actually on the team walking out in front of the fans. Chin up and carry your neck stretched elegantly tall!

Make eye contact with every judge on the panel, smiling at each one as if he or she were an old friend you were excited to see. Truly CONNECT with your eyes. You can even wink at a judge or two but don't overdo it!

Take your start place on the floor with a final flourish, such as sharply drawing your leg into the beginning pose. As you stand waiting for the music, many of the judges will be evaluating your appearance and body, so make sure to stand in a flattering pose of power and not meekly or shyly. Judges want to know how you will act when you are just walking around or standing at promotional events, not just when you are dancing. That's why your demeanor during non-dancing portions of the tryout is so important.

What to do if you forget the choreography

Commonly, a candidate will lose concentration or her memory will fail during the performance. This can be caused by any number of distractions or even just stress and fear. Sometimes it becomes a domino effect, with one dancer losing her steps and causing the other dancers to falter as well.

If this happens to you, try your best to keep your face positive and confident. Pose in a flattering position long enough to get your bearings, then catch up to the routine. If you are completely at a loss, then just start over from the beginning or from where you left off and keep dancing as if no one else is on the floor with you.

The judges are looking for confidence and the ability to keep your cool, so do your best to stay composed no matter what happens, and to recover as best you can from any memory lapses.

How to exit in a way that maximizes your score

No matter how much you want to run off the floor as fast as you can after your time in the limelight ends, do not give in to that flight instinct! When you strike the final pose, you will probably feel elation, relief, mortification, or a combination of those and similar emotions. If you prepared for your audition well by following the prep advice in this book, hopefully you will feel only elation and no mortification! But feeling relieved is a given.

But despite your relief, do not slump into relaxation mode when you end your performance. Keep that confident and dazzling smile on your face, and connect again with each judge with your eyes. Wait patiently for the person cuing the candidates to release you or your group from the floor before moving off. Stand in a flattering pose while you wait, similar to a pose you would see on a team headshot, such as standing with one leg slightly bent and one hand on your hip.

When you are released, walk off with confidence, gliding off stage similarly to how you entered. Remember, you are always on stage, even when the music stops, and even after you have walked off.

BONUS SECTION: After the audition

Walking out of the audition room doors will feel GREAT. One way or the other, you did it! You conquered your doubts, fears, and insecurities and showed up with courage. You gave it your all, and lived life fully for the hours you endured the strange and exhausting world of auditioning for a pro dance team.

Sometimes, you will be told whether or not you made the team on the same night as the audition. Other times, a team might announce the results later, such as the next day. So you might walk out of that door knowing whether you made the team, or with some butterflies in your stomach due to the anticipation of finding out whether your tryout resulted in success.

Here are some tips for you, whether you made the team or not.

If you make the team

Congratulations! Your hard work paid off, and luck was on your side as well. Your efforts resulted in your dream coming true, and you can now proudly call yourself a professional cheerleader.

Be sure to comply with any directions from the team as to whether you are allowed to publicly disclose to family and friends that you made it onto the team, or if you have to wait until a certain time or event, such as an announcement on the team website. Your social networking announcements should also comply, so do not post any photos of auditions unless you know you have permission to do so.

Your team director will let you know about any next steps, such as training dates, rehearsal logistics, and schedules. Work hard to be the type of cheerleader that the director can depend on, and be a good role model to everyone around you. Next year, be sure to help another aspiring candidate to live HER dream by serving as a mentor to her! And please email your good news to email@ArenaCheerleader.com and you might be featured in a future interview!

Best wishes! You are now on your way to one of your life's most exciting adventures!

If you do not make the team

If you auditioned and did not make the team, then your confidence probably took a huge blow.

I can honestly relate. I was cut twice at the auditions for my dream NFL® dance team before making it my third time. The disappointment each year I was cut was so strong it felt like a physical stomach ache!

It's odd how debilitating rejection can be. The key is to keep trying, until you no longer want that goal. If you want to be a professional cheerleader, then you keep auditioning and improving until you make it. Don't worry, your journey doesn't end unless you want it to!

It is the nature of the business that you will not be selected for everything you audition for; there are just too many dancers out there, and not enough team spots!

If you want feedback, which I encourage you to seek, you can send an email to the team director a week or two after the audition. Include a copy of your application and a photo of yourself to remind the director who you are, and ask if he or she would be willing to give you a few pointers for the following year's audition. Be positive, appreciative for the director's time, and don't be pushy or demanding. In general, it is appropriate to do this only if you made it to the final round.

Failure tests our character more than anything else. Your response after a disappointment matters more than anything. What you do next is your choice, but I hope you choose to keep trying.

Remember: *"Success is falling nine times and getting up ten."* ~ Jon Bon Jovi

BONUS SECTION: Do not let fear get in your way!

Do you know that many dancers "chicken out" the night before or morning of auditions and don't show up, even if they prepped and planned to? Are you worried you might lose your nerve and be a no-show that morning?

Do not let fear get in your way! Remember that the audition will be great practice for you no matter what, even if you didn't prep as fully as you meant to.

Ask yourself: What is there to lose? What are those possible outcomes? Mere rejection? Are you willing to risk that? You might find that the rewards outweigh the risks. The possible rewards should give you the courage to show up.

If you were paralyzed, or sick in bed with chronic disease, or in prison, or living somewhere else, or any other myriad of reasons why this weekend's auditions might not be an option for you, then you wouldn't have a choice.

But if you are reading this book, then I'm guessing that you DO have a choice. You are likely one of the few people in the world who has this opportunity open to you. You are in the right place, at the right time, with the right training.

Does your heart want you to take advantage of the fact that you can go to this audition? Do you really want to pass that up? Ask yourself and answer yourself honestly. Put fear aside.

Whatever you decide to do, I salute and support you for choosing this journey. My heart travels with all dancers who embark on this difficult yet worthwhile adventure. A part of me will be out on that audition floor with you!

I wish you every bit of luck in the world, and I hope to meet you in person someday at one of my live bootcamps or a book signing. Cheers!

Best regards always,
Flavia

What next?

Do you feel alone in this journey? Well, you aren't alone! There are so many other women just like you who are dreaming of cheering for the pros and are on the same journey as you to achieve that goal.

Join these other inspiring women at a bootcamp or retreat soon! Simply join the book mailing list at www.ArenaCheerleader.com.

On the website, you can access the "book extras" downloads and join the free mailing list to periodically receive:

- Info about retreats and bootcamps where you can meet other aspiring pro cheerleaders and form lifelong bonds!
- Choreography videos
- Tips & tricks
- Audition news
- Interviews with current pro cheerleaders
- Spotlight articles on team directors
- Announcements about new books and editions
- Discounts from companies who want you to try their makeup, nutrition, and other products
- Healthy recipes
- News and articles about the pro cheer world

Thanks again for purchasing this book and good luck at auditions!

Cheers!

Need your help with Amazon!

If you love this book, please don't forget to leave a review at **Amazon.com**! Your review will help make the next edition even better! Every one of the reviews is read, and it really means a lot to get feedback from you, the reader. Success stories are the best of all!

If you left a review on Amazon for this book, simply forward the email from Amazon confirming that your review went live to receive a FREE 15-minute Q&A telephone call with Flavia Berys herself or one of her alumni pro cheerleader community members!

Just forward your Amazon review confirmation email to:

email@ArenaCheerleader.com

and someone will get back to you within 72 hours to schedule your telephone appointment!

Thanks again for purchasing this book and good luck at auditions!

Cheers!

www.ingramcontent.com/pod-product-compliance
Lightning Source LLC
Chambersburg PA
CBHW060849050426
42453CB00008B/919